INTRODUCTION

Before you read any further, try this: Flip through this book *from back to front*. While you're flipping, watch the upper right-hand corner. Cool, huh? Are you ready to learn how to do this yourself?

Animation has got to be one of the greatest art forms ever invented. You don't just get to make a great drawing—you get to bring it to life. You might think that most of the animation you see today is made by computer. But in fact almost all of today's animated TV shows, from *Spongebob Squarepants* to *The Powerpuff Girls* to anime (Japanese animation), are drawn the old-fashioned way, by hand.

Hand-drawn animation, also known as "2-D animation," is at the heart of almost every good animated film or TV show. Even computer-animated movies need animators to draw the ideas and characters by hand before they can be computerized.

Christopher Hart's Animation Studio will show you how animators bring their ideas to life. It's like a behind-the-scenes tour of your favorite animated show! You'll start in the cartooning workshop, where you'll get tips on drawing cartoon characters. Next is the animation department. Here you'll learn the secrets of animation—techniques like anticipation, squash and stretch, and double bounce. And in the special effects and lay-out departments, you'll see how animators plan scenes, create cool backgrounds, show funny actions, and more.

At the end of the book there's a special bonus: instructions for making a simple flip book so you can bring your own animated character to life! So what are you waiting for? Let's get animating!

CHRISTOPHER HART

THE CARTOONING WORKSHOP

Animation is a series of drawings, one after the other, each slightly different from the one before. When it's drawn well, animation is like music to the eyes. Animators are artists—they have to be. With little more than a pencil, they must convince the audience that their cartoon actors are real.

Animators draw on special animation paper, which is punched with holes to fit snugly onto a peg bar that keeps the pages lined up. The peg bar is part of an animation disk. A light shines up from the animator's desk through the clear disk, lighting up the paper so the animator can see through many layers of drawings at the same time.

If the animation paper isn't held firmly in place by the pegs, a slight shifting will occur from drawing to drawing, making the animated image jump and flutter. People would throw popcorn at the screen. Raisinets would go flying. What a mess.

This is an animation disk. Professional animators use these to hold their drawings.

The first drawing has the dog standing still. The next one shows the dog with his paws up in the air, getting ready to place his paws on his hips. In the last drawing, he completes his task. These are "key drawings," or "extremes." Several drawings must be added between these extremes to make the action flow smoothly.

CREATING A CHARACTER

Before we begin to animate, let's learn how to draw animated cartoon characters.

Your character must be built so that it can be drawn in lots of poses. It's best to make your character "round" because as he moves, he turns, and as he turns, he must seem to be round. Flat characters are dull and lifeless. Notice, too, how elastic this face seems. It's ready to stretch into all kinds of expressions.

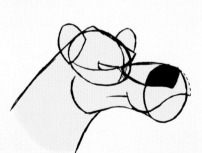

Animals, like people, are drawn step by step.

BIG SHAPES AND SMALL SHAPES

This lady is a rather large character. But instead of giving her a big nose and big eyes, I've gone in the opposite direction. I've given her small features: tiny eyes, a normal-sized nose, and tiny ears.

On the other hand, if this character were skinny, it would work better to give her larger features. By contrasting big with small, you can make your characters more interesting.

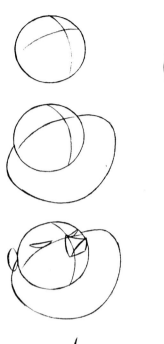

USING WEIRD HEAD SHAPES

This character is a tough guy—you can tell by his massive neck. But instead of giving him an equally massive chin, I've given him a long, thin jaw. The long jaw contrasts with the small, compact skull on top.

You can create an interesting character like this by simply changing parts of a "normal" head shape.

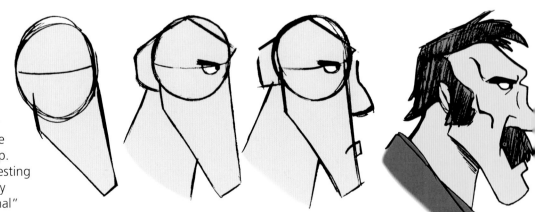

THE CHARACTER'S BODY

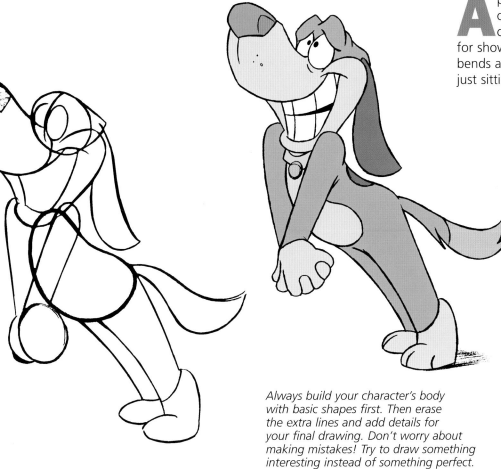

A pear-shaped body is one of the best for animated characters. It is also good for showing emotions. The torso bends and stretches; it is never just sitting still.

Always build your character's body with basic shapes first. Then erase the extra lines and add details for your final drawing. Don't worry about making mistakes! Try to draw something interesting instead of something perfect.

DRAWING FROM ALL ANGLES

It's important to build your character's body first before going to the finished version. This helps you see exactly how the character is built, so you can turn her around while keeping her body proportions the same. A great-looking character is useless if it can't be redrawn from many angles.

Notice how the bottom of the shirt curves?

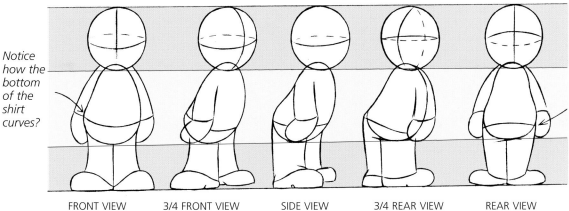

FRONT VIEW   3/4 FRONT VIEW   SIDE VIEW   3/4 REAR VIEW   REAR VIEW

See how the front of the shirt curves down but the back of the shirt curves up? This makes it look like the character is leaning forward. A pose is more interesting when it is leaning, and not perfectly centered.

BODY SIZES

Just because you're using the pear shape doesn't mean that every character's body has to look the same. Try changing the size and shape of the pear to create a never-ending cast of characters.

Different body types inspire different feelings. A puppy's body might make you feel soft and mushy, while a bully's body might make you feel scared. When creating a character, it is always important to match body type to personality.

When the pear shape is turned upside down, you get a tough-guy character, which is the typical personality of the cartoon bull.

The teenager is a carefree type. His body is lanky and loose. Therefore, stretch out the pear shape to make it more narrow.

A short pear, with a heavily arched back, is good for young, innocent characters such as this puppy.

DRAWING IN THREE DIMENSIONS

As you practice drawing characters, try thinking of them as three-dimensional, with form and substance to their bodies. Draw the body with basic, solid shapes. When the body looks solid, add the clothes. This two-step approach—drawing the body first, and the clothes second—is what sets the pros apart from the amateurs.

ACTION LINE

This character is based on an egg shape. Most of his weight is in his lower body, which causes his knees to bend as he shuffles along.

7

EXPRESSIONS, EMOTIONS, AND REACTIONS

Here's an experiment for you. Draw an angry face from your imagination. Next, go to a mirror, make an angry face, and draw what you see.

The second drawing is no doubt better. Using a model is a tradition in art. The mirror is a great tool because it allows you to be your own model.

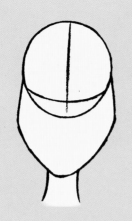

Drawing the basic face

SAD

CONFIDENT

HAPPY

JEALOUS

SURPRISED

ANGRY

BODY ATTITUDES

Beginning cartoonists often think that the face is where a character's expression is created. Foolish mortals! That's only partly true. Suppose a character was smiling, but he was standing with his shoulders hunched over. He wouldn't look happy—he'd look like his heart was broken and he was just putting up a good front.

Bodies show emotion just as much as faces do. In the top examples, you can tell what each emotion is without any faces at all. These bodies are based on human anatomy, rather than on the pear shape.

SAD   PROUD   HILARIOUS   ANGRY   SNEAKY   STUBBORN

"REALISTIC" BODY

For a character that looks a little more realistic, this simplified body works well.

It helps to get some experience drawing actual people. You can practice by drawing friends, family, even people sitting in a park or waiting at your bus stop.

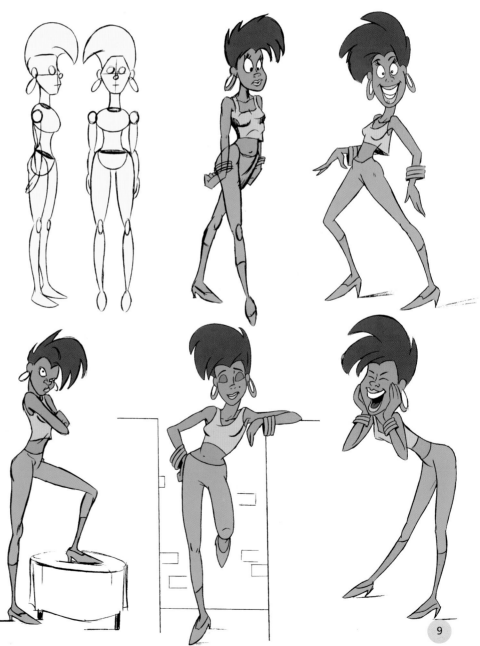

LOTS OF POSES FROM ONE DRAWING

You've drawn a pose. "Not bad," you think, "but I can do better." Here's a way to fix your drawing without starting from scratch. First, make changes to your original drawing without erasing. Then compare the old pose to the new one. Which do you like better? Or maybe something between the two is best? Pick the one you want, then trace over your rough for a final, clean version.

This technique works well if you only want to move the head and torso.

This approach does NOT work when you want to change the legs. When you change the legs, the entire body shifts position. The head, shoulders, and hips move, too, and suddenly you have a whole new pose.

By just changing the arms, we give this character two different poses.

This cat can lower its head to the ground or perk up and look behind itself, all from the same drawing.

EXAGGERATION

Animation is big on exaggeration. The "mild" poses in the first column are okay, but the "medium" poses in the second column are better. And the "extreme" poses in the third column are by far the best. Always go for the big emotions!

THE TIRED WALK

MILD   MEDIUM   EXTREME

THE RUN

MILD   MEDIUM   EXTREME

THE REACTION

MILD   MEDIUM   EXTREME

THE PUNCH

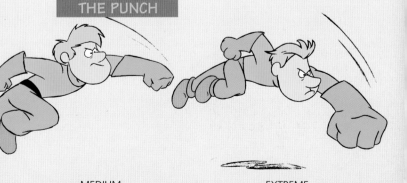

MILD   MEDIUM   EXTREME

THE ANIMATION DEPARTMENT

Welcome to the animation department! Now you'll learn how to transform your cartoon characters into moving, living actors. Store these techniques in your head and use them when you need them. They'll work for all characters, from the simplest to the most advanced.

ANIMATOR'S BRAIN

FLOW AND INERTIA

SQUASH AND STRETCH

ANIMATING ON AN ARC

ANTICIPATION AND TIMING

TRIPS TO THE FRIDGE

ANTICIPATION AND SQUASH AND STRETCH

Before a character makes any big action, he must first draw back in the *opposite direction*. This is called *anticipation*.

Before jumping, this character *anticipates* by squashing down. Notice that when he *squashes* down, he becomes wider and shorter. When he jumps up he *stretches*, becoming longer and thinner. This is called *squash and stretch.*

This bear is going to walk forward. But before he takes a step forward, he *anticipates* by rearing back.

1   **2**   **3**   **4**

This magician wants to cast a spell from his fingertips. Before he can lunge forward, he must raise his fingertips in anticipation. But the anticipation move is so big in and of itself that it requires its *own* anticipation. The motion goes like this:
1. Character is ready.
2. Short anticipation downward.
3. Big anticipation up.
4. Final move.

INERTIA

I'm not talking about wanting to stay in bed after the alarm clock rings—this is a different type of inertia. Think of the character or object as being sort of flexible and very heavy. When the character or object moves, it *drags* itself from wherever it was before.

BODY FIGHTS INERTIA

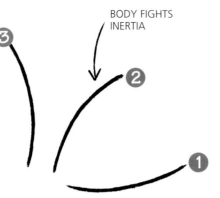

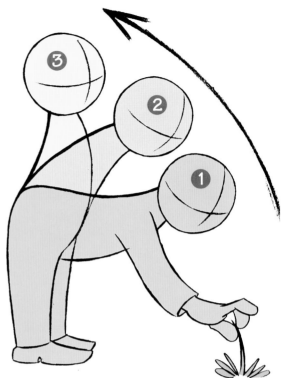

As the man stands up, he drags his body upward (1). In the second position (2), his body is still feeling the inertia of being pulled up. In the third position (3), he has recovered and is standing straight up.

The flagpole lies flat on the ground. When the hand lifts it up, the ends of the pole drag behind.

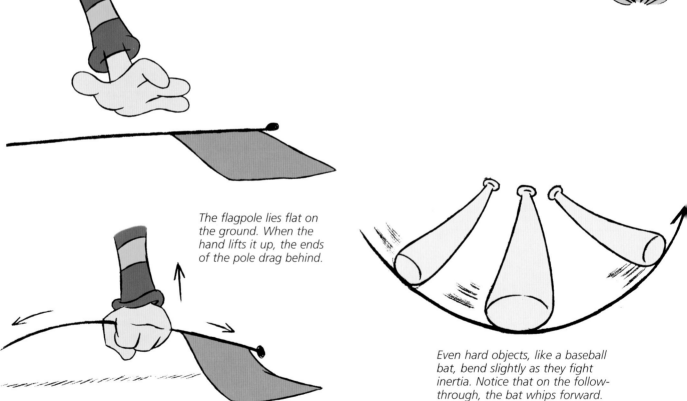

Even hard objects, like a baseball bat, bend slightly as they fight inertia. Notice that on the follow-through, the bat whips forward.

EXTREMES AND IN-BETWEENS

EXTREME

IN-BETWEEN

EXTREME

The first drawing and the third drawing both look like normal expressions, right? But drawing number two does not. It goes in between the first two, which is why it's called an *In-between*. The first and third drawings are solid expressions. They are called *extremes*.

An animator always draws the extremes first, to capture the essence of the scene. The extremes are then handed over to a less experienced animator, called an in-betweener, who draws the in-betweens to connect the extremes.

Pretend you're an in-betweener. The animator has given you two drawings: extreme number 1 (the top drawing) and extreme number 5 (the bottom drawing). That means the animator expects this motion to take five drawings. But he's only given you the two extremes. How do you know what to draw?

The animator expects you to come up with three drawings so that the scene goes as follows: extreme number 1, in-between number 2, in-between number 3, in-between number 4, extreme number 5.

To begin, you would first figure out the middle in-between. Since there are three in-betweens (2, 3, and 4), the middle in-between is number 3. This is called the *breakdown drawing*.

Next, you would place drawing number 1 (the first extreme) over drawing number 5 (the second extreme) and draw a pose halfway between the two. This is the breakdown drawing (in-between number 3).

You would then place drawing number 1 (the first extreme) over the breakdown drawing (in-between number 3), and draw a pose halfway between them. This would become in-between number 2. You would then do the same with drawings 3 and 5 to get in-between number 4.

In-betweening is a good beginning job in animation. Young in-betweeners learn a lot and can move up the ranks quickly.

To make a smooth, pleasing motion, an action should follow an arc. Without an arc, the hand would jump up and down as it moved. Arcs are used to smooth out many kinds of actions, such as kicking or throwing a ball.

The arc is drawn first; the animation follows it.

Remember inertia? No matter which direction the hand moves, the sleeve lags behind.

TIMING

We all move at different speeds at different times. Some actions are slow; others are fast; some speed up while others slow down. Poor animation shows every action at the same speed. This makes it look as though the character is walking in a jar of molasses.

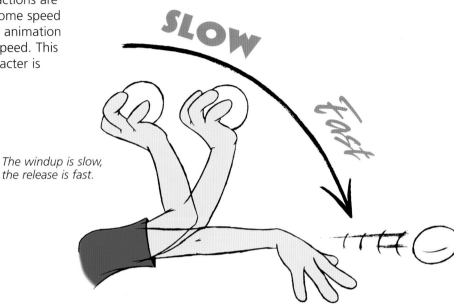

SLOW

Fast

The windup is slow, the release is fast.

SLOW

FASTER

FASTEST

A GOOD RULE OF THUMB:

Always make some actions move faster than others. This will make your animation look more realistic.

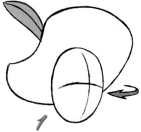

1
Head is still.

Part of the fun of animation is watching objects flow from one place to another. This usually involves a *secondary* action. A secondary action is one that comes out of a first, bigger action, like the ripples that form after you throw a pebble in the water.

Here, the first action is the face turning. The secondary action is the feather following.

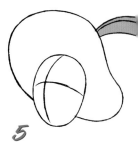

5
Feather is in new position.

2
Feather dips as head begins turning to the left.

3
Feather now begins to turn.

4
Top half of feather still trails, while bottom half has moved over to new position.

DOUBLE BOUNCE

Remember our old friends, squash and stretch? After an object squashes, it bounces back up (it stretches). But if it were to stop at that point, it would look frozen.

Objects in animation slow down *gradually*. They don't come to a sudden halt. An object can bounce several times on its way to regaining its original form.

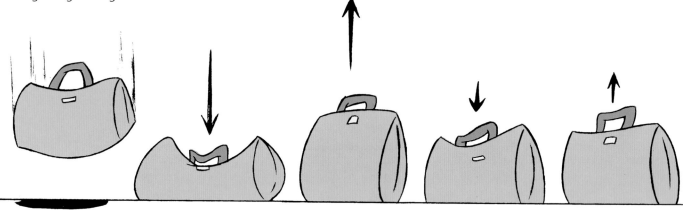

1
Suitcase falls.

2
Heavy squash.

3
Big stretch.

4
Small squash.

5
Small stretch back to original position.

**A**NIMATION

et's see how all of this works in actual animation. Notice the secondary actions of the book and the glasses.

1

Elephant reads book on creaky stool.

5

Begins first bounce up (stretch).

2

Stool gives way, elephant stretches as he falls.

CRACK

6

Stretch continues.

3

Begins to squash as he hits the floor.

7

Bounces back down (small squash).

4

Continues to squash.

8

Bounces back up to original position.

THE WALK CYCLE

1

2

3

The right leg lands in full stride.

The right leg begins to slide back as the left leg begins to lift off.

The left leg crosses. The right leg continues to slide back.

7

8

9

Repeat the moves above with the opposite leg.

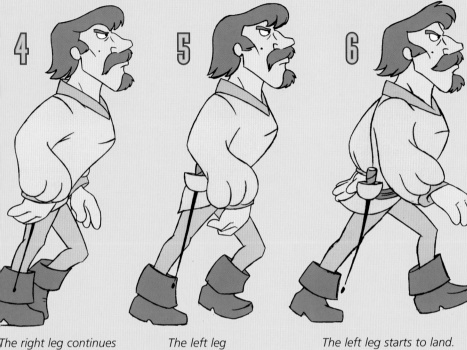

L and, sink, slide back, push off, lift up, recoil, repeat. These are the basic steps each leg goes through during the walk. This is called a *walk cycle*.

It takes about twelve drawings to make your character take two steps. The twelfth drawing would then go back to drawing number one, creating a continuous motion without beginning or end. You can repeat the walk cycle as long as you want.

The right leg continues to slide back.

The left leg moves forward.

The left leg starts to land.

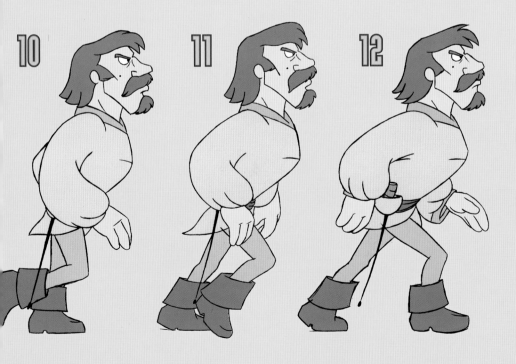

CHARACTER WALKS: TWO KINDS

Once an animator has finished drawing the character and background, the drawings are scanned into the computer. They are then layered so that the character appears on the top layer, and the background layer is underneath. Here are two ways animators use layers to show a character walking forward.

STRAIGHT AHEAD WALK

This character is moving forward as he walks. The background doesn't move at all. Each character drawing shows him moving to the right. If you were to continue the walk, the character would walk right off the page.

CHARACTER MOVES AHEAD

CHARACTER WALKS PAST THE BACKGROUND

PANNED WALK

If your character will be walking for a long time, here's an easier way to make it look like he's moving forward. Draw the same walk cycle, but without moving your character to the right. Instead, slide your background drawing to the left each time he takes a step. This will make it look like he's walking forward.

BACKGROUND IS PULLED UNDER THE CHARACTER, WHO WALKS IN PLACE

THE CARTOON RUN

After the push-off, both legs are off the ground.

This heavy character squashes as he lands. Notice also the *inertia* of the tails of his jacket— as the man lands, the tails drag behind. The character stretches as he gets ready to leap again.

This is a *half cycle*. In other words, only the first half of the run is shown. For a complete cycle, you would need more steps for drawing 6 to hook up to drawing 1.

FOUR-LEGGED ANIMAL WALK

1

2

Pretty much all four-legged animals—horses, dogs, lionesses—have the same walk cycle. Practice running your eyes quickly past these drawings so that you can "see" the lioness animate.

3

4

5

HOW THE LIONESS WALKS

The lioness takes a step with each leg on one side, followed by a step with each leg on the other side.

If she starts with her left side, the left rear leg goes first, followed by the left front leg.

Now that she's moved both of her legs on the left side, naturally, she must move the legs on the right side. She will move her right rear leg first, followed by her right front leg.

The walk cycle goes like this:

A. Left rear leg

B. Left front leg

C. Right rear leg

D. Right front leg (then repeat)

The hard part comes between these steps. As one leg is landing, the other legs are either sliding back, lifting, crossing over, or getting ready to land. Only *one foot* hits the ground at a time.

6

7

8

A CLOSER VIEW: THE LIONESS WALK

've numbered each foot in the order in which they move. It's easy if you remember that the left side goes first (rear foot, front foot) and the right side goes second (rear foot, front foot).

As the head lifts, the angle of the head tilts up as well.

As the head dips, the angle of the head tilts down.

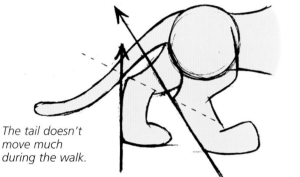

The tail doesn't move much during the walk.

THE REAR LEGS

As the rear leg moves back, the foot becomes more vertical (see arrows).

THE HEAD AND SHOULDERS

Our body parts are all connected. When the lioness lifts a front leg, her left shoulder dips down because it is no longer being held up by the leg. It's as if you removed a pillar that was holding up a roof. Take the pillar away, the roof sags. Same thing with the shoulder. As the shoulder dips, the head dips, too.

The opposite happens when the lioness puts her front leg down on the ground—the shoulder is pushed up, and the head rises. To make it short and sweet: When she raises her front leg, her head dips. When she plants her front leg, her head rises.

BIRDS IN FLIGHT

You can really see the inertia on a bird's wings when it flies. The wings bend gently with each stroke.

HOW BIRDS RISE AND FALL IN FLIGHT

The bird rises and falls slightly with each stroke. As the bird lifts its wings, it begins to fall, because gravity has taken over. As the bird flaps down, it rises again.

This is a good exercise to draw in a flip book (see page 46 for more about flip books). You can draw a bird as simple as the lines above. Notice how the bird rises and falls above and below the line as it flies.

PLANNING A SEQUENCE

Before you begin to animate a scene, it's a good idea to sketch out the general poses, just to see if the scene works well.

1

This hungry guy is about to chow down on a juicy burger.

2

But that taste! He stops in the middle of chewing. His eyes grow big, making him look surprised.

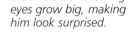

3

He spits it out.

4

He recovers with a nice sip of coffee.

5

Another stunned reaction. His eyes become tiny dots.

6

He spits it out again!

BREAKING THE RULES OF REALITY

Cartoon characters live in worlds where anything is possible! The only limit is your imagination.

The cat chases a bird off a cliff. Only a cartoon character would fail to notice that she is running off a cliff!

2

The cat, having lost the bird, freezes in midair. She still hasn't realized there's no ground beneath her. And notice that she has somehow managed to run several steps in midair before stopping.

3

She looks down, sees there's nothing below her, and does a take in which her body rises even more in the air.

4

She looks at the audience for sympathy and waves a pitiful goodbye.

5

This is a technique called snap and fall. Her body reacts to gravity one section at a time, with lots of stretch.

6

A smoke cloud appears with speed lines as the cat falls into the water. A big splash should follow.

THE SPECIAL EFFECTS DEPARTMENT

THE ANIMATED "TAKE"

1

*The sheriff looks.
He sees something.*

2

*He crouches down in
anticipation of the take.*

A *take* is a big reaction to something, like when the cat on pages 28–29 realized she was floating in midair. There are three parts to the take:

1. *Anticipation.* The character must really coil down in order to spring into the take.

2. *Take.* The reaction should be super exaggerated. Arms and legs are stretched to the max.

3. *Recovery.* The character goes back to normal. Finish with another pose.

3

*A huge take. His
hat flies off, his neck
stretches, his hair
drags behind. His
near hand gets bigger,
as if it was closer to
the camera lens.*

4

*The character begins
to recover. He floats
back to the ground.
His hat falls back
on his head.*

5

End with a new pose.

NUTTY TAKES

This is how the mouth looks during a take. The top half looks like a smile, but the bottom half looks horrified.

HAIR TAKE
Always think about your character when planning a take. This hair take works great for a lion, but you wouldn't use it for a shorthaired dog.

EYEBALL TAKE
It's not just the eyes that are flying off this character, but his ears and tongue as well. They all go back to normal as he recovers.

OFF-THE-GROUND TAKE
It can be funny to make your character lift off the ground during a take. The arms and legs are stretched out from the body and the tail is straight. Notice how the fur ruffles.

SPEED LINES AND OTHER FUN THINGS

When you want an action to look like it's happening really fast, try using *speed lines*. The speed lines must disappear immediately after the action has happened.

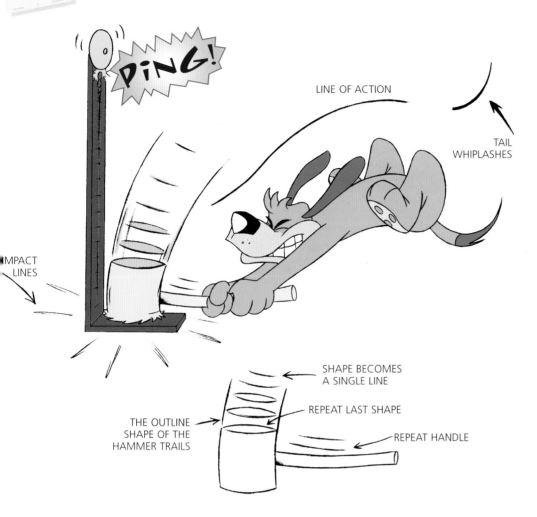

DING!

LINE OF ACTION

TAIL WHIPLASHES

IMPACT LINES

SHAPE BECOMES A SINGLE LINE

THE OUTLINE SHAPE OF THE HAMMER TRAILS

REPEAT LAST SHAPE

REPEAT HANDLE

CURVED SPEED LINES
Speed lines can curve at the end. This works well with characters that have been standing still. Give these speed lines a brushed feeling, not a hard ink line.

TWO WAYS TO DRAW SPEED LINES

All the speed lines are together in one bunch.

Speed lines are in smaller bunches at many places.

THE LAYOUT DEPARTMENT

It's the layout person's job to figure out the best way to stage (or "lay out") a scene before it goes to the animator. Here is a scene in which three kids find a treasure chest in the woods. One way to stage the scene is to have the three kids running, one after the other, for the treasure (top drawing). But there are also other ways to draw the scene. For instance, one of the kids could have found the treasure and calls to the other two (middle drawing). Or the kids could be so excited that they fall all over each other trying to get to it (bottom drawing). There are lots of ways to lay out any scene.

PLACING YOUR CHARACTERS

By changing the way your characters are placed, you say a lot about what is going on in the story.

BOY IN FRONT

If the boy is at the head of this crocodile family, it tells the audience that wherever they are going it is the kid's idea. Mother is next. Dad is trailing last, reluctant to go. This gives you an idea of who's in control: mom and her kid. Because the characters are lined up from smallest to tallest, it makes it easy for the eye to move from one to the other.

BOY IN THE MIDDLE

Whatever is planned for the afternoon, the kid wants no part of it. He is trapped in the middle.

BOY IN BACK

This shows that the grownups are in one world, the kid in another. This kid was probably goofing off instead of getting ready, and as a result, he's late. As in the first drawing, the line of sight goes in one direction, this time from tallest to smallest.

COMPOSING A SCENE

It's best to organize a scene before you start drawing the characters. One trick is to use triangles. A triangle can help you place your character in the center of the scene (such as at right). It can also help group different elements together (below). And it can give shape and direction to objects that are so close together they might otherwise be confusing to look at (below, right). Always erase the triangle before doing your finished drawings.

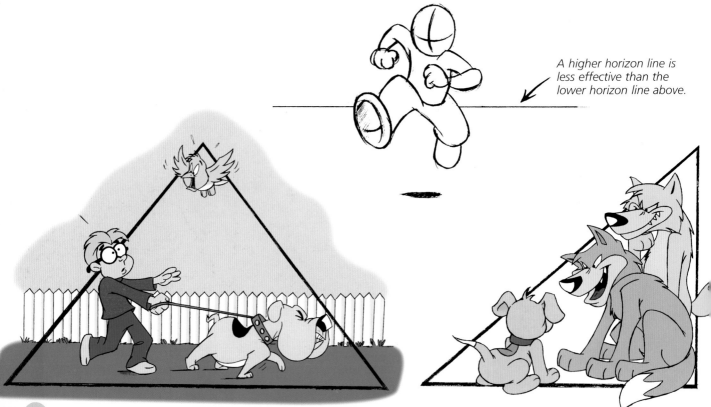

A higher horizon line is less effective than the lower horizon line above.

Here are some principles of a good layout.

This horizontal "frames" the scene...

...so does the vertical.

There's empty space for the eyes to rest.

Diagonals create energy between characters.

More empty space for the eyes to rest.

ATTACKING A SCENE

If I asked ten people to draw a man standing in a doorway, I would probably get ten drawings with a guy standing in the middle of a doorway, at eye level. The drawings would look nice, but what would they mean? Not much. You see, no one would have asked the important questions *before* starting to draw: What is going on in the story? What are they trying to show in the scene? You can't draw until you know *why* you are drawing. Then you should attack the scene with everything you've got.

LAYOUT TRICKS

SHADOWS

Add shadows underneath your characters to give them a feeling of weight and reality. Shadows can also be used to show that one character is bigger and stronger than another.

The gorilla's shadow covers the smaller character.

HIDDEN SHAPES

When you draw two characters together, try to find a hidden shape in the space between them. This is called *negative space*. Negative space is the shape of the space *between* objects.

This negative space looks like an upside-down vase.

CHOOSING AN APPROACH

Let's take a story idea and choose a layout for the first scene. Suppose we want to show a log cabin in the woods, with a bad guy prowling about.

Layout number 1 shows how most people might draw the scene. The drawing is nice, but it doesn't make a *statement* about what's going on. We have no idea what's going to happen.

Layout number 2 is better. By making the house small, with two large legs in the foreground, we get a sense that something bad is going to happen. But the house might belong to the man whose feet we are seeing.

For all we know, he might be coming home from work. It's not very clear.

Layout number 3 is best. We can tell that he is a bad guy from his expression. And we see that he is approaching the house with only bad intentions.

Layout number 4 shows too much detail for the first scene. We can't tell how big or small the cabin is. And we can't see that the cabin is all by itself in the woods, which is important for building suspense. This layout would work well as a follow-up shot to layout number 3.

THE LANGUAGE OF FILM TECHNIQUES

When you draw animated scenes, you are really making movies. So it helps to understand how movies and movie cameras work. If a movie showed every scene exactly the same way, the film would be really boring. Here are some other ways to show scenes. Look at the pictures on page 41 for an example of each.

A. ESTABLISHING SHOT: EXTERIOR
Sets an outdoor scene from a distance.

B. ESTABLISHING SHOT: INTERIOR
Sets the scene inside, showing the characters and their relationships.

C. FULL SHOT
A drawing of someone, including the entire head and body.

D. MEDIUM SHOT
A drawing that includes the head and chest (see dotted line) or the head, chest, and part of the legs.

E. CLOSE-UP SHOT
A drawing of the head, or of the head and shoulders.

F. EXTREME CLOSE-UP
Very close on the face.

G. TWO-SHOT
A drawing that shows two people.

H. REVERSE ANGLE
A two-shot in which one character stands with his back to the camera. The character facing the camera should be slightly smaller because she is farther away.

I. PANNING
Panning is when the camera seems to move from left to right or from right to left. Actually, the camera doesn't move at all—it's the drawing that moves. In this scene, the camera starts by focusing on the dog. To show who the dog is running after, we *pan* to the rabbit by "pulling" the drawing to the left until the rabbit is under the camera.

J. CAMERA SHAKE
To make it seem like the earth is shaking, the camera shifts to the left, then to the right, then a little bit less to the left, then to the right, then even less to the left, and so on, less and less until the shaking stops.

K. TRUCK IN
The camera moves toward the animation to get a closer view of something.

L. TWIST IN
The animation turns as the camera trucks in. This is especially good for scary scenes.

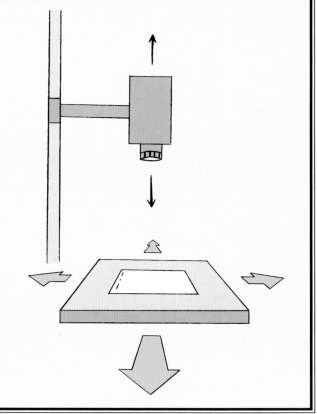

HOW ANIMATION IS SHOT

The drawings are placed on a platform, with a camera focused down on them. Two frames of film are clicked off for each drawing, which is then replaced by another drawing. (Each *second* of an animated movie takes twelve drawings!)

The camera can only move up or down (closer to the drawings or farther away). The closer it is to the drawings, the larger the animation will look on screen. The platform moves in four directions, as shown below.

HOW THE BACKGROUNDS MOVE

Ever notice that when you're riding in a car, the things nearby seem to whiz past while the hills in the distance creep by? The nearer an object is to the viewer, the faster it seems to move. The farther away an object is, the slower it seems to move. It's the same in animation. To show this dog walking, the animator has drawn him walking in place while moving the background drawings beneath him. This makes it look like the dog is walking forward. Moving the background this way is called *panning*. The larger arrows show which parts of the background have faster pans. The smaller arrows show slower pans.

FANTASTIC SETTINGS

In live action movies, it is very expensive to shoot "on location." If you had a story that took place in France, it would cost an arm and a leg to fly everyone to France and pay for them to stay there.

But in animation, it costs no more to draw a background of the Eiffel Tower than to draw anything else. You can choose any setting that makes sense for the story, no matter how crazy or fantastic.

CAVERN TO THE CENTER OF THE EARTH

You can even draw a castle in the sky, or in a galaxy far, far away.

Castle in the Sky

TWO WAYS TO DRAW PATHWAYS TO INFINITY

FOR A CAVERN AT THE CENTER OF THE EARTH

FOR A CASTLE IN THE SKY

1. Start with a winding road that ends in a point.

1. Draw two sets of lines like this.

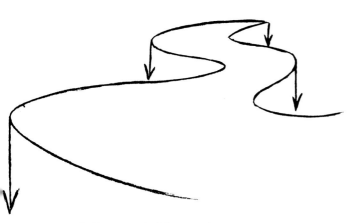

2. Draw vertical lines at the turns.

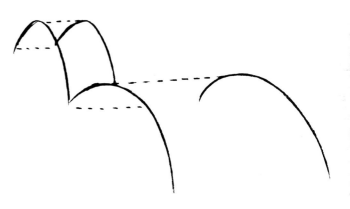

2. Connect the highest points and the lowest points.

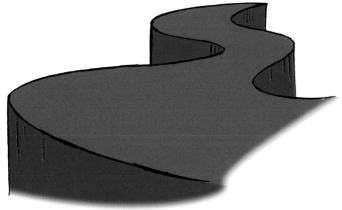

3. Shade the curved areas.

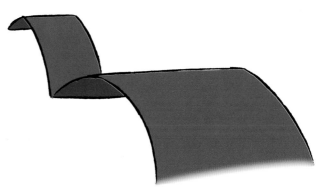

3. Fill in the path. Erase the extra lines.

MAKING A FLIP BOOK

When I first became interested in animation, I loved the flip books I got at Disneyland. I was fascinated by how the animation would spring to life. I would stop, mid-flip, and study the changes from drawing to drawing.

It's easy to make your own flip book. Just go to any stationery store or drugstore and buy a small pad of blank white paper (without lines). Small pads are best.

Now you're ready to start filling the pad's pages. First, think about what you want to animate. A cat walking? A person jumping? How will you lay out the drawings? Turn to pages 47 and 48 for some ideas.

Once you've decided on a sequence, do your *first* drawing on the *last* page of the pad. Draw darkly. Then, flip over the page before it, so there is a blank page on top of your drawing. Trace your first drawing onto the blank page, making small changes as you go. This then becomes the second drawing in your sequence. When you're done, flip another page over and do the same, tracing your second drawing onto the new page and again making small changes. Keep going until you have a series of drawings.

To test your drawings, use your thumb to flip through the book *from back to front*. You will probably want to change some of your drawings to make the animation flow smoother. Don't worry if you make a mistake! Animation is a process of trial and error. Professional animators make many attempts before choosing one approach.

When you've finished, stand back and admire!

Regular people usually flip from front to back.

Animators always flip from back to front.

Draw darkly so you can trace each drawing onto the next piece of paper.

If you want to show a figure moving across the page, draw horizontally so there's enough room.

CREATING SIMPLE FIGURES FOR YOUR BOOK

It's best to start by drawing simple characters. Once you see that your animation works, go back and fill in the details.

Don't draw stick figures—you won't be able to tell which is the front leg and which is the back leg.

See how you can't tell which leg is which?

This simple character would work well in a flip book.

CAP

GLOVE

USING CHARACTER MARKERS
Your eye needs something to follow from drawing to drawing. Add "markers" (like a baseball glove or a vest or a hat) to make your character easier to follow.

HAIR

BELT

SKIRT

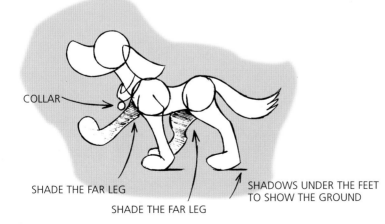

COLLAR

SHADE THE FAR LEG

SHADE THE FAR LEG

SHADOWS UNDER THE FEET TO SHOW THE GROUND

VEST

FLIP BOOK IDEA LAB

Here are a few ideas for your flip book. If you want, try adding in-between drawings to make the animation smoother. You might also want to try some of the walks and runs we've learned about in this book.

DROP OF PAINT ON BALL

MAN "CRACKING UP"

STAIRS BECOME A SLIDE

PULL BACK FROM A SCREAM

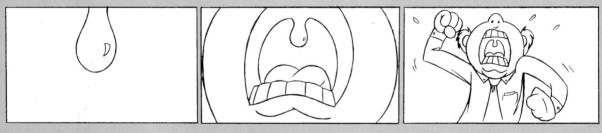

MAN MORPHING INTO A WOLF